POPULAR
SONGS
HAL LEONARD
TUDENT PIANO LIBRARY

D0503931

Elton John

Arranged by Carol Klose

Cover photo © Photofest, Inc.

ISBN 978-1-4234-3416-0

7777 W. BLUEMOUND RD. P.O. BOX 13819 MILWAUKEE, WI 53213

Visit Hal Leonard Online at
www.halleonard.com

CONTENTS

Can You Feel the Love Tonight

from Walt Disney Pictures' THE LION KING

Music by ELTON JOHN
Lyrics by TIM RICE
Arranged by Carol Klose

when the heat ___ of the roll - ing world can be turned a - way. ___
that the twist - ing ka - lei - do - scope moves us all in turn. ___

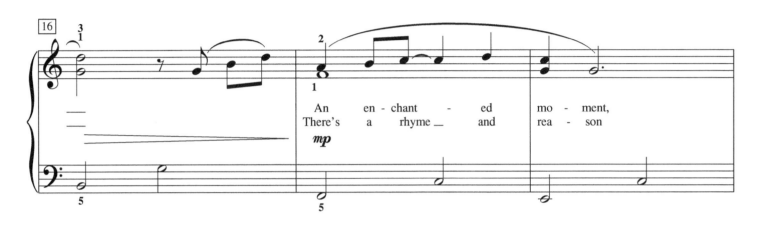

An en - chant - ed mo - ment,
There's a rhyme ___ and rea - son

mp

and it sees ___ me through. ___ It's e - nough for this
to the wild ___ out - doors _____ when the heart of this

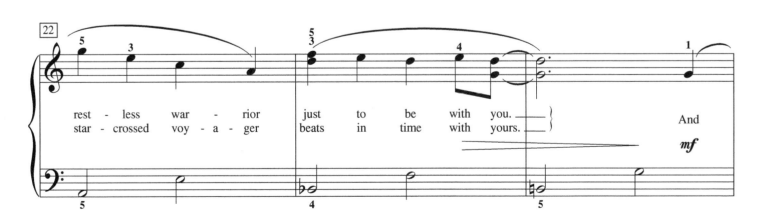

rest - less war - rior just to be with you. ___ And
star - crossed voy - a - ger beats in time with yours. ___

mf

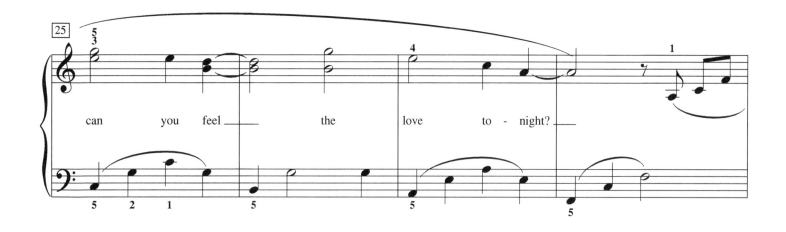

can   you   feel _____   the   love   to - night? _____

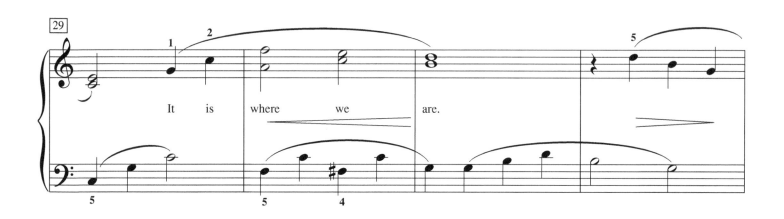

It   is   where   we   are.

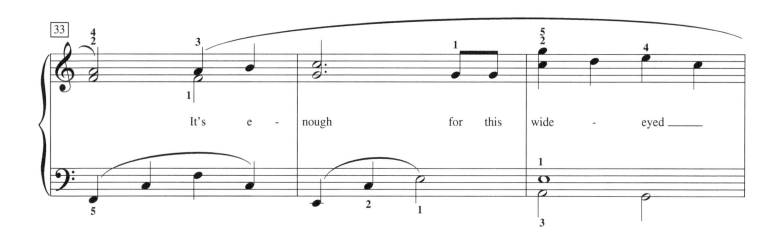

It's   e - nough   for this   wide -   eyed _____

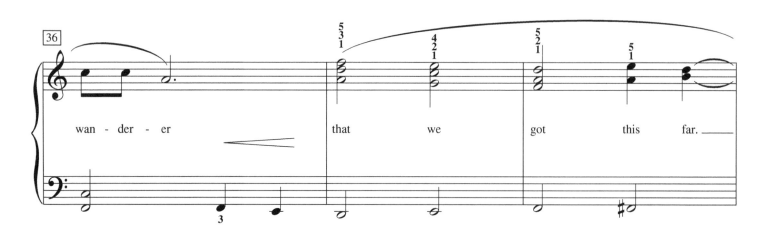

wan - der - er _____   that   we   got   this   far. _____

And can you feel

the love to - night, how it's

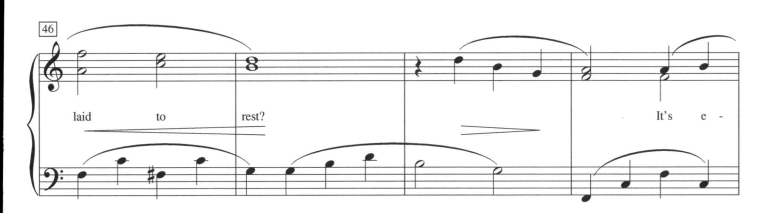

laid to rest? It's e -

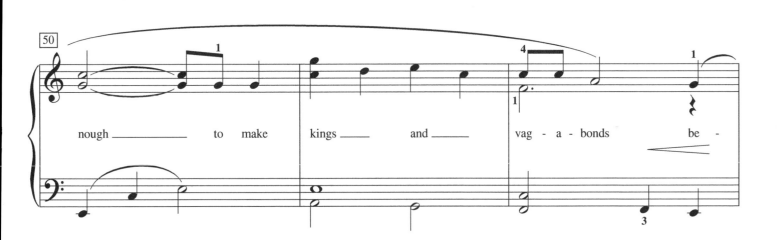

nough to make kings and vag - a - bonds be -

7

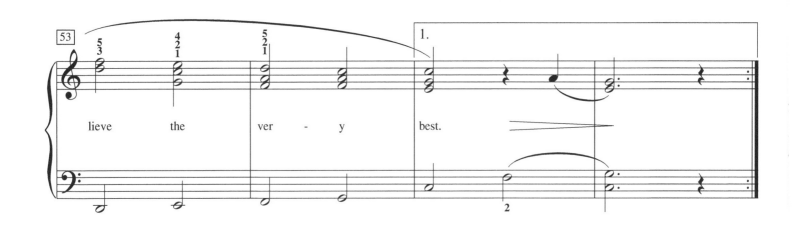

lieve   the   ver   -   y   best.

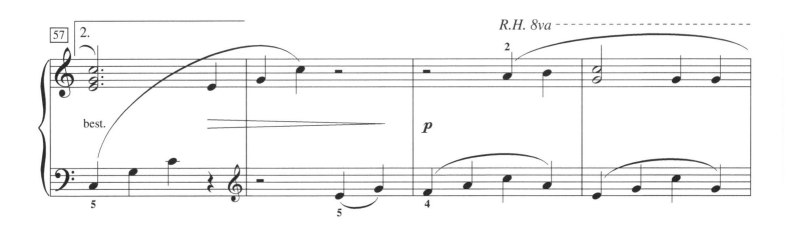

best.

R.H. 8va - - - - - - - - - - - - - - - - - - -

p

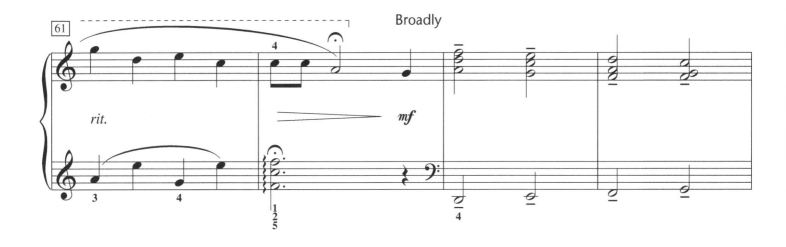

Broadly

rit.

mf

rit.

R.H.

p

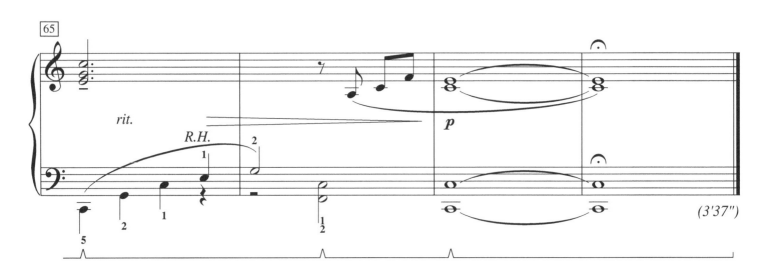

(3'37")

Candle in the Wind

Words and Music by ELTON JOHN
and BERNIE TAUPIN
Arranged by Carol Klose

Gently ($\quarternote$ = 88)

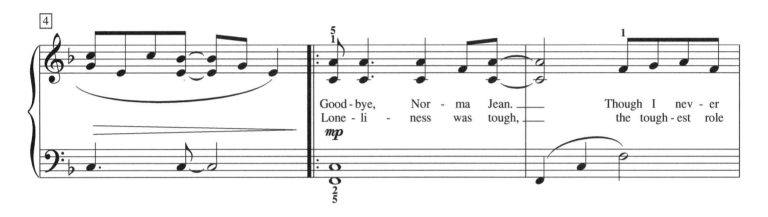

Good - bye, Nor - ma Jean.___ Though I nev - er
Lone - li - ness was tough,___ the tough - est role

knew you ___ at all, you had the grace to
you ev - er played. Hol - ly - wood cre - at - ed a

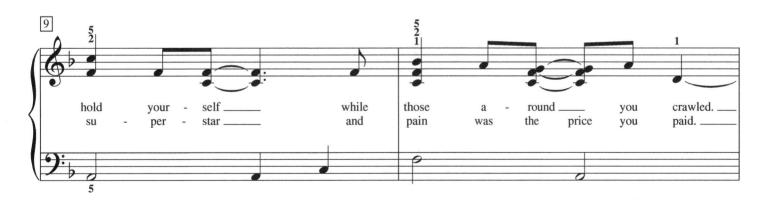

hold your - self ___ while those a - round ___ you crawled.
su - per - star ___ and pain was the price you paid.

They crawled out of the wood - work
And e - ven when you died,

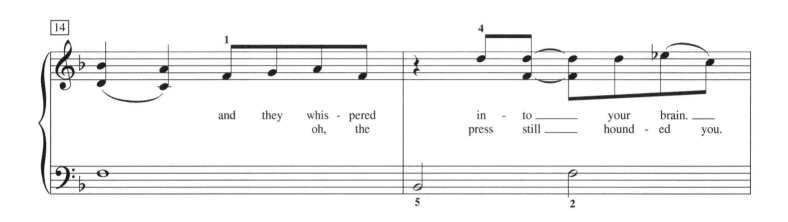

and they whis - pered
oh, the

in - to your brain.
press still hound - ed you.

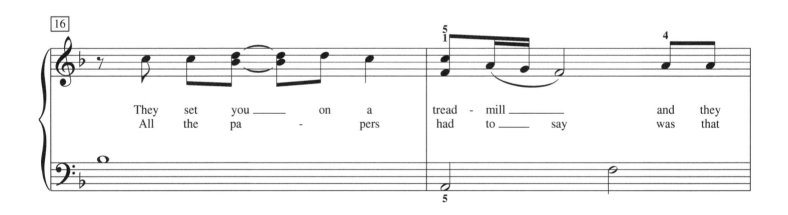

They set you on a
All the pa - pers

tread - mill and they
had to say was that

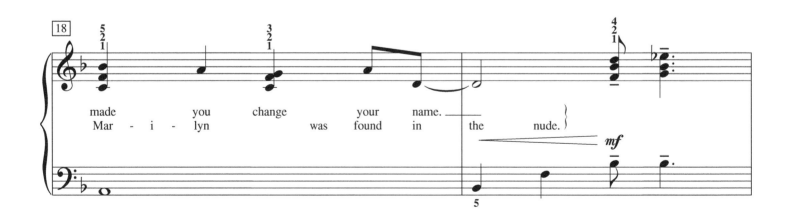

made you change your name.
Mar - i - lyn was found in the nude.

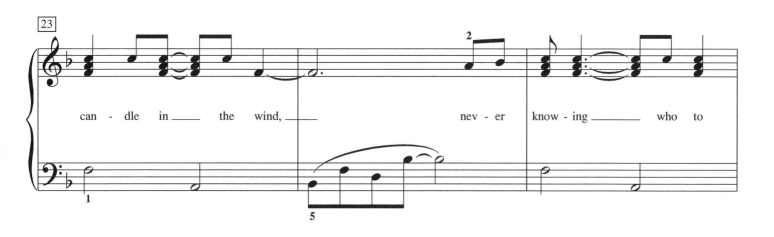

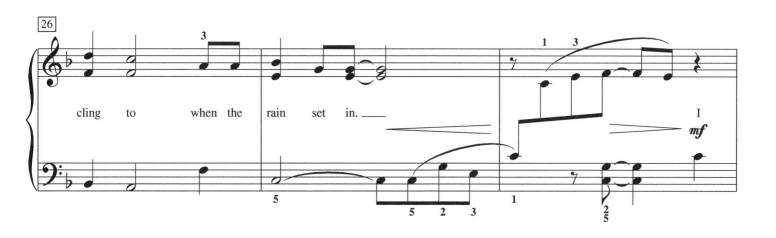

can - dle burned _ out   long   be - fore ___   your

leg - end   ev - er   did. ___

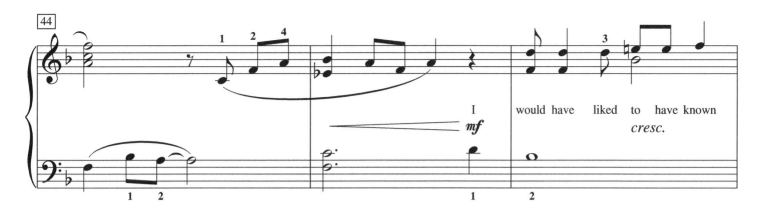

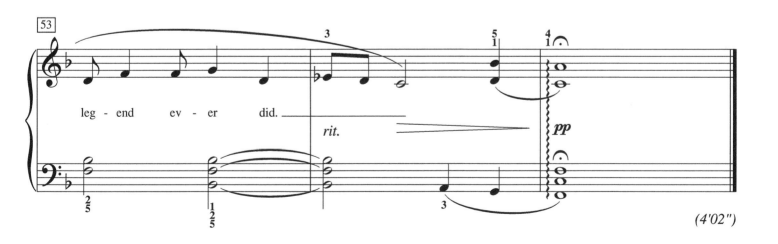

I would have liked to have known you, oh, ___ but I ___ was just a kid. Your can - dle burned out long ___ be - fore ___ your leg - end ev - er did. ___

(4'02")

Crocodile Rock

Words and Music by ELTON JOHN
and BERNIE TAUPIN
Arranged by Carol Klose

With a light-hearted Rock beat (straight 8ths) (♩ = 120)

(1.,3.) I re- mem- ber when rock was young.
(2.) years __ went by and __

__ rock just died. Me and Su- sie had so much fun __ hold- in'
Su- sie went and left me for some for- eign guy.

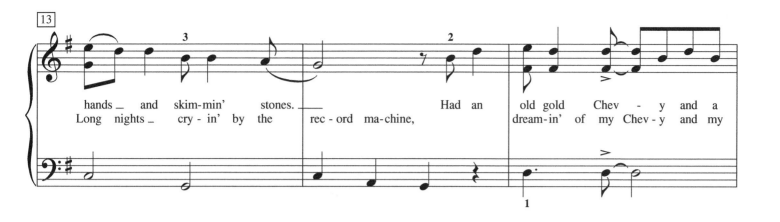

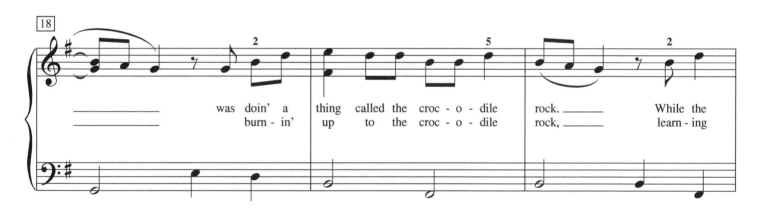

15

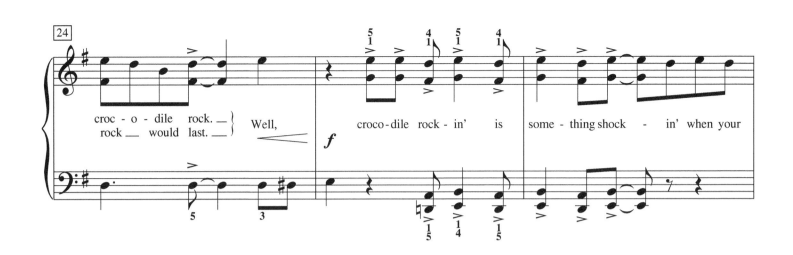

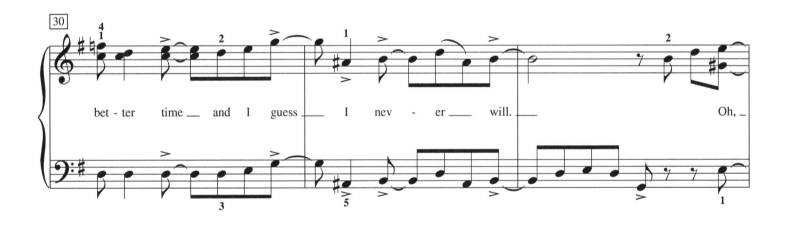

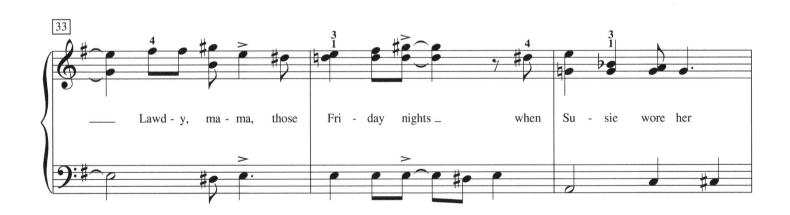

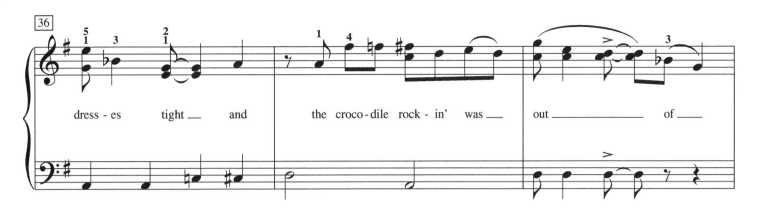

dress - es tight ___ and the croco - dile rock - in' was ___ out ___ of ___

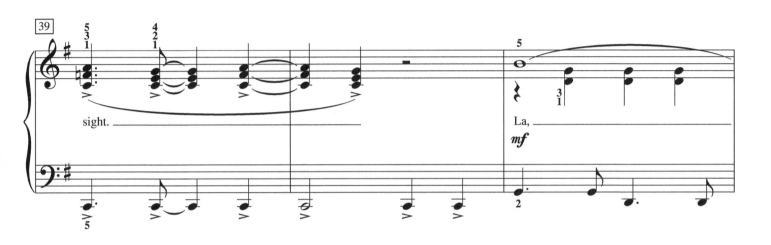

sight. ___ La, ___

la la la la la, ___ la la la la

la, ___ la la la la la.

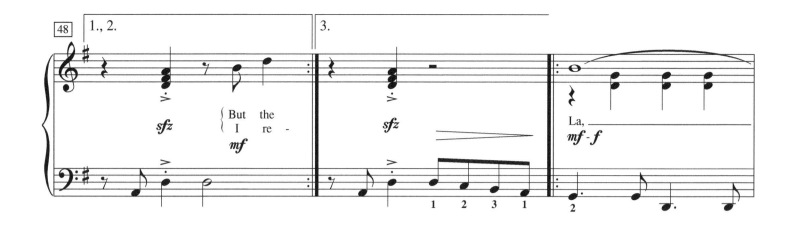

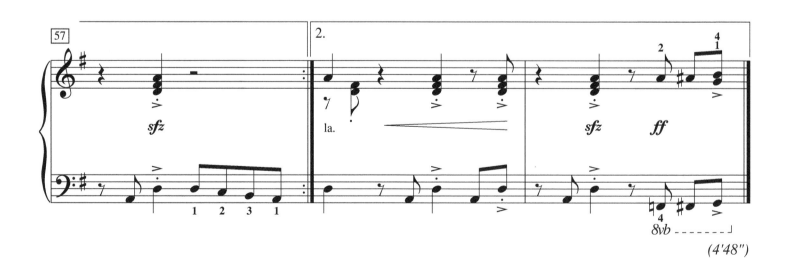

(4'48")

18

Tiny Dancer

Words and Music by ELTON JOHN
and BERNIE TAUPIN
Arranged by Carol Klose

Moderately, with a steady beat (♩ = 120)

Blue - jean ba - by. ___
Je - sus freaks ___

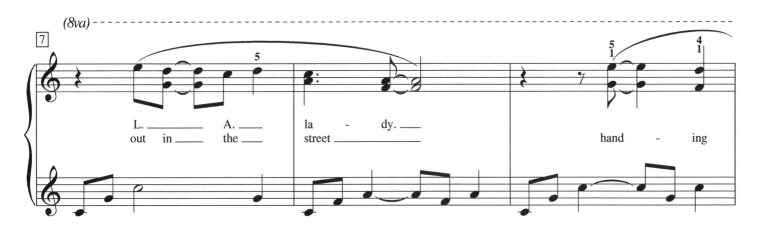

L. ___ A. ___ la - dy. ___
out in ___ the ___ street ___

hand - ing

Seam - stress for the band. _____

tick - ets out for God. _____

cresc.

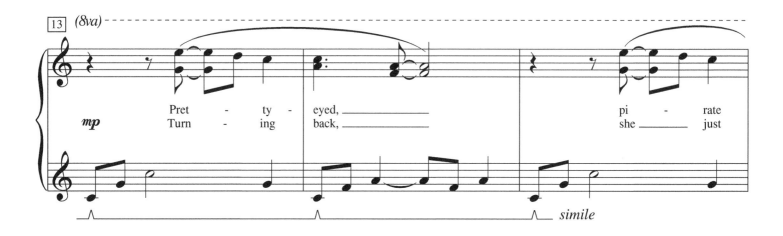

mp

Pret - ty - eyed, _____ pi - rate

Turn - ing back, _____ she _____ just

simile

smile, _____

laughs. _____

you'll mar - ry a mu - sic

The boul - e - vard is not that

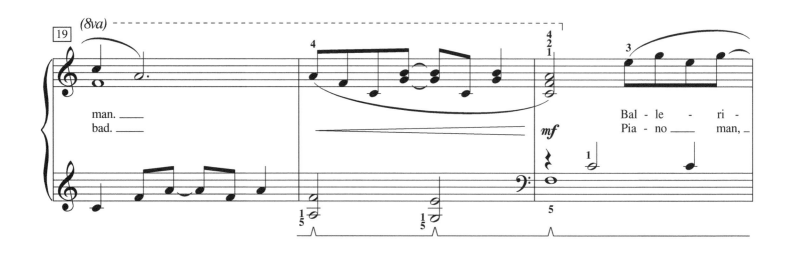

man. _____

bad. _____

mf

Bal - le - ri -

Pia - no _____ man, _____

-na.

You must ___ have seen her ___
he makes ___ his stand ___

_∧_ *simile*

in the

danc - ing in the sand. ___
au - di - to - ri - um. ___

And now ___ she's in me, ___
Look - ing on, ___

mp

al - ways ___ with me, ___ ti - ny
she sings the ___ songs. ___ The word she ___

danc - er   in   my
knows, the   tune she
hand. _____
hums. _____

But, oh, how it feels ___ so   real   ly - ing here   with

no one near.	On - ly you, _____ and you ___ can

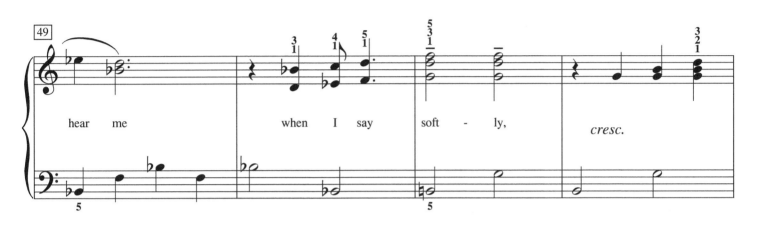

hear me	when I say	soft - ly,	*cresc.*

slow - ly:	*f*	Hold me clos -

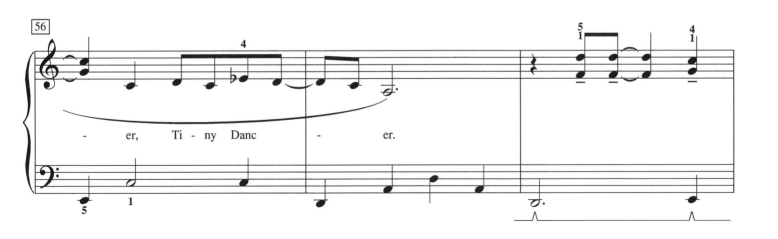

- er,	Ti - ny Danc -	er.

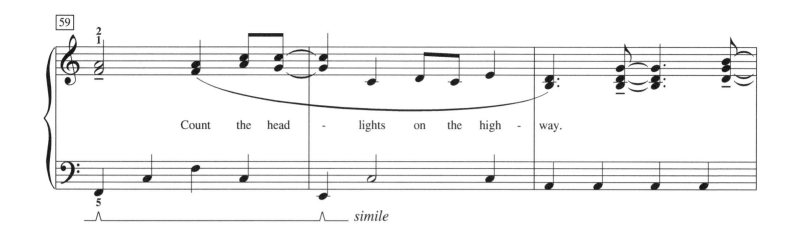

Count the head - lights on the high - way.

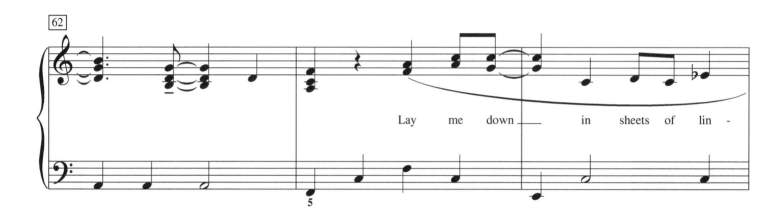

Lay me down___ in sheets of lin -

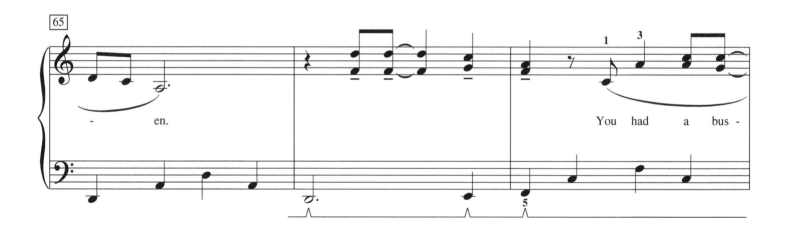

- en. You had a bus -

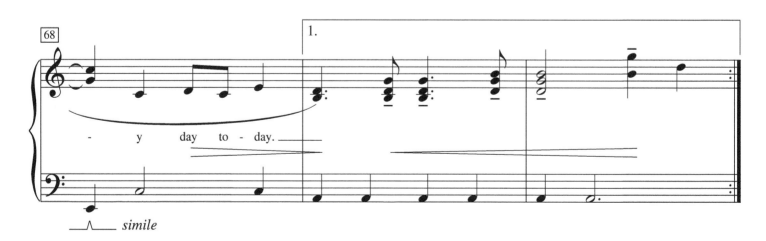

- y day to - day.___

simile

(4'22")

Goodbye Yellow Brick Road

Words and Music by ELTON JOHN
and BERNIE TAUPIN
Arranged by Carol Klose

know you can't hold ___ me for - ev - er, ___ I did - n't sign up ___ with you. ___
May - be you'll get ___ a re - place - ment, ___ there's plen - ty like me ___ to be

___ found. I'm not a pres - ent for your friends to o - pen, this
Mon - grels ___ who ain't got a pen - ny, ___

boy's too young ___ to be sing - ing the blues. ___
sniff - ing for tid - bits like you on the ground. ___
mf

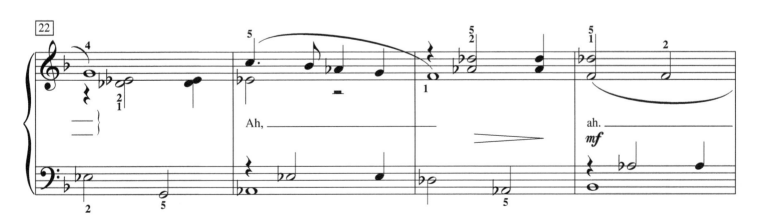

Ah, ___ ah. ___
mf

27

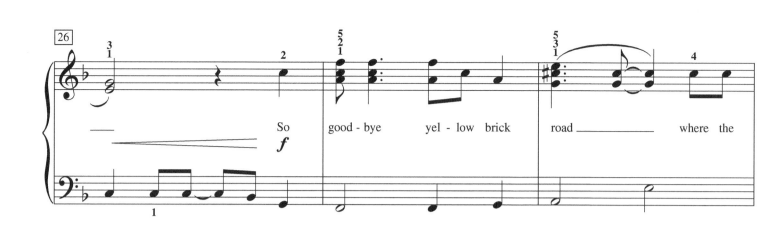

So good-bye yel-low brick road _____ where the

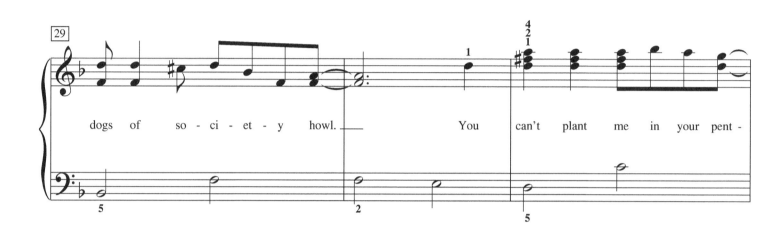

dogs of so-ci-et-y howl. _____ You can't plant me in your pent-

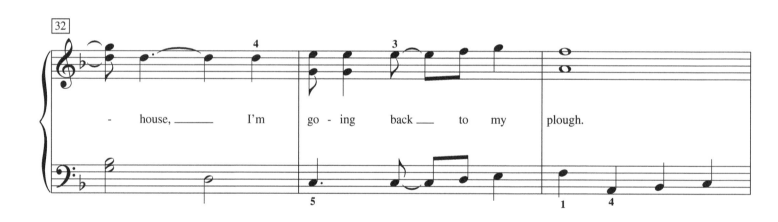

- house, _____ I'm go-ing back ___ to my plough.

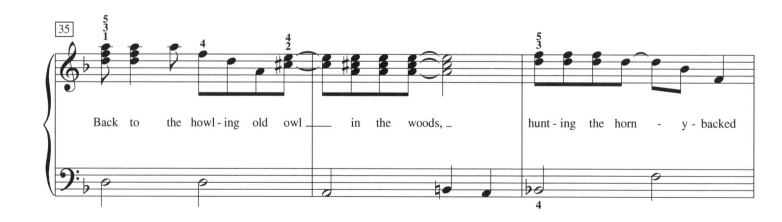

Back to the howl-ing old owl ___ in the woods, __ hunt-ing the horn - y - backed

Sorry Seems to Be the Hardest Word

Words and Music by ELTON JOHN
and BERNIE TAUPIN
Arranged by Carol Klose

What have I got to do ___ to make you care? ___

What do I do to make you

want me?

What have I got - ta do ___

to ___ be heard?

What do I say when it's ___ all o - ver?

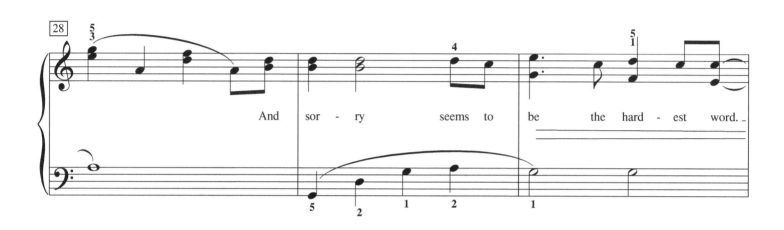

And sor - ry seems to be the hard - est word. _

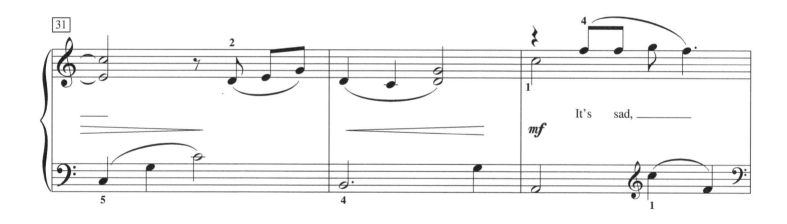

It's sad, _____

it's so sad. ___ It's a sad, sad sit - u - a - tion, _

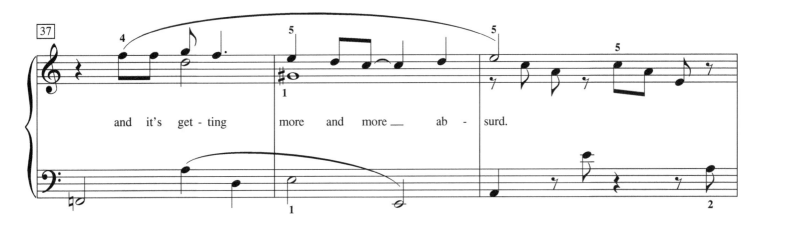

and it's get - ting more and more___ ab - surd.

mf It's sad,_____ it's so sad.___

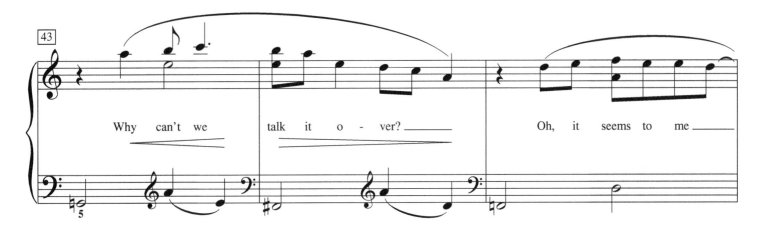

Why can't we talk it o - ver?_____ Oh, it seems to me___

___ that sor - ry seems to be the hard - est

poco rit.

(2'42")

Your Song

Words and Music by ELTON JOHN
and BERNIE TAUPIN
Arranged by Carol Klose

Moderately, with feeling (♩ = 120)

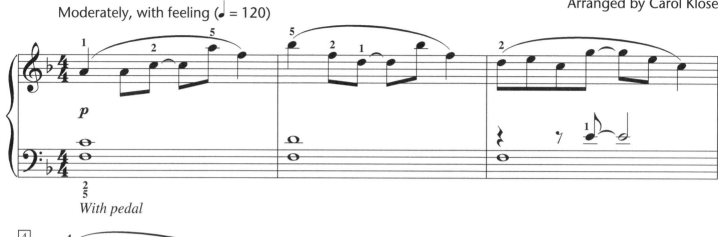

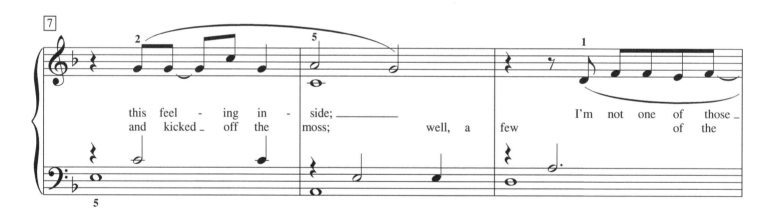

I don't have ___ much mon - ey, ___ but,
But the sun's been quite kind ___

boy, if I
while I wrote this

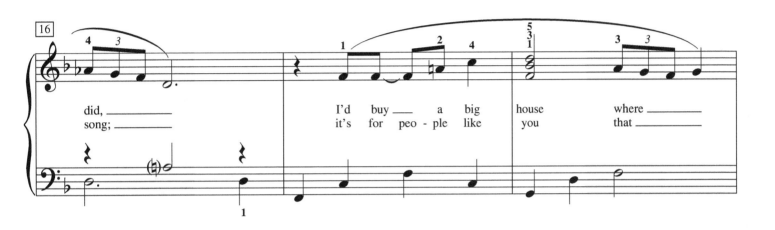

did, ___
song; ___

I'd buy ___ a big house where ___
it's for peo - ple like you that ___

we both ___ could live.
keep it ___ turned on.

If I were a sculp - tor, ___
So ex - cuse me for - get - ting, ___

mf

but then ___ a - gain, no, _____ or a man _____ who makes po -
but these ___ things I do; _____ but, you see, _____ I've for-got-

- tions in a trav - el - in' show. _____ I
ten if ___ they're green or ___ they're blue. _____

know ___ it's not much but it's the
An - y - way, ___ the thing _____ is,

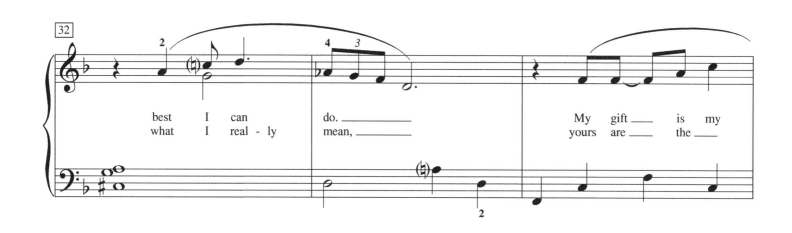

best I can do. _____ My gift ___ is my
what I real - ly mean, _____ yours are ___ the ___

song, and _____ this one's __ for you. _____

sweet - est eyes _____ I've ev - er seen. _____

_mf_ And you __ can tell ev - 'ry - bod - y __

__ this is your song. _____ It may __ be

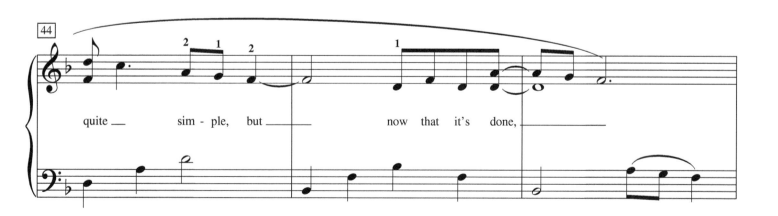

quite __ sim - ple, but _____ now that it's done, _____

I hope you don't mind,_____ I hope you don't mind_____ that I put_____ down in_____

cresc.

words   how   won - der - ful   life   is _____   while

f   *mp*   *rit.*

1.

you're __ in _____ the world. _____

a tempo

2.

you're __ in _____ the world. _____

a tempo

(4'04")

Written in the Stars

from Elton John and Tim Rice's AIDA

Music by ELTON JOHN
Lyrics by TIM RICE
Arranged by Carol Klose

Moderately slow, with feeling (♩ = 56)

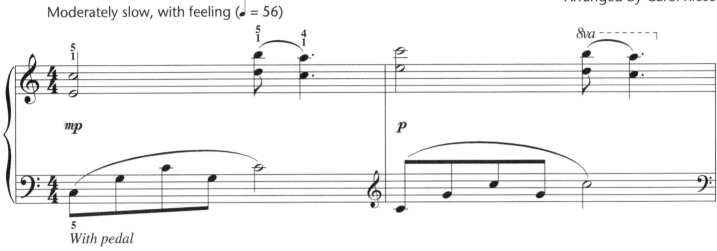

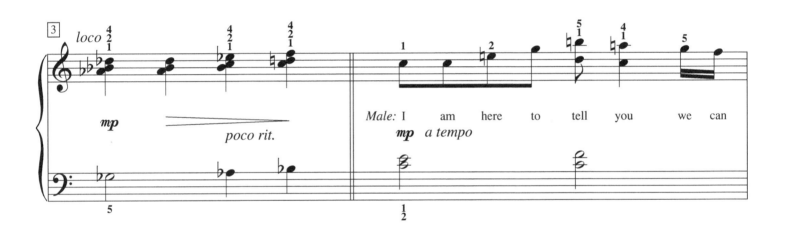

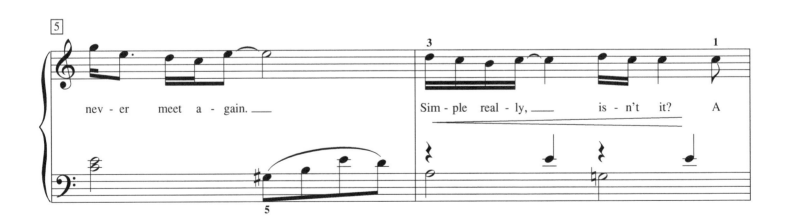

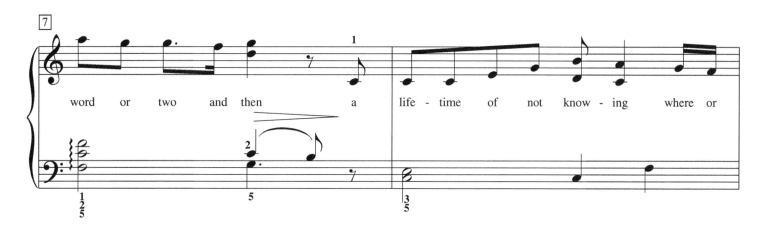

word or two and then a life - time of not know - ing where or

how or why or when. ___ You think of me or speak of me or

cresc.

won - der what be - fell the some - one you once loved so long a -

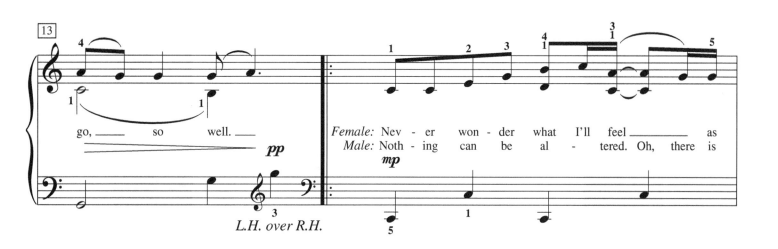

go, ___ so well. ___

pp

L.H. over R.H.

Female: Nev - er won - der what I'll feel ___ as
Male: Noth - ing can be al - tered. Oh, there is

mp

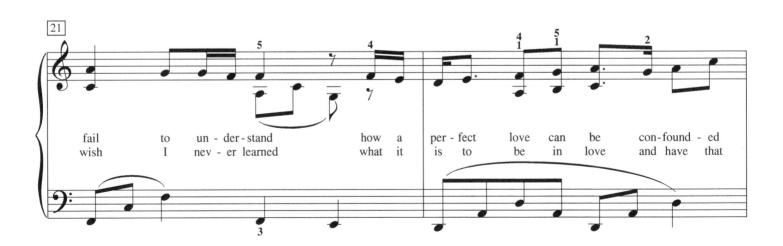

out of hand. _____
love re - turned. _____ } *Both:* Is it writ - ten in the stars? Are we

mf

pay - ing for some crime? Is that all that we are good for, just a

stretch of mor - tal time? _____ Is this God's ex - per - i - ment in

which we have __ no say, in which we're giv - en par - a - dise, but

on - ly for a day?

on - ly for a day?

dim.

p
rit.

pp

(3'58")

POPULAR SONGS

HAL LEONARD STUDENT PIANO LIBRARY

The **Hal Leonard Student Piano Library** has great songs, and you will find all your favorites here: Disney classics, Broadway and movie favorites, and today's top hits. These graded collections are skillfully and imaginatively arranged for students and pianists at every level, from elementary solos with teacher accompaniments to sophisticated piano solos for the advancing pianist.

Adele
arr. Mona Rejino
Correlates with HLSPL Level 5
00159590.............................$12.99

The Beatles
arr. Eugénie Rocherolle
Correlates with HLSPL Level 5
00296649.............................. $12.99

Irving Berlin Piano Duos
arr. Don Heitler and Jim Lyke
Correlates with HLSPL Level 5
00296838.............................$14.99

Broadway Favorites
arr. Phillip Keveren
Correlates with HLSPL Level 4
00279192.............................$12.99

Chart Hits
arr. Mona Rejino
Correlates with HLSPL Level 5
00296710.............................$8.99

Christmas at the Piano
arr. Lynda Lybeck-Robinson
Correlates with HLSPL Level 4
00298194.............................$12.99

Christmas Cheer
arr. Phillip Keveren
Correlates with HLSPL Level 4
00296616.............................$8.99

Classic Christmas Favorites
arr. Jennifer & Mike Watts
Correlates with HLSPL Level 5
00129582.............................$9.99

Christmas Time Is Here
arr. Eugénie Rocherolle
Correlates with HLSPL Level 5
00296614.............................$8.99

Classic Joplin Rags
arr. Fred Kern
Correlates with HLSPL Level 5
00296743.............................$9.99

Classical Pop – Lady Gaga Fugue & Other Pop Hits
arr. Giovanni Dettori
Correlates with HLSPL Level 5
00296921.............................$12.99

Contemporary Movie Hits
arr. by Carol Klose, Jennifer Linn and Wendy Stevens
Correlates with HLSPL Level 5
00296780.............................$8.99

Contemporary Pop Hits
arr. Wendy Stevens
Correlates with HLSPL Level 3
00296836.............................$8.99

Cool Pop
arr. Mona Rejino
Correlates with HLSPL Level 5
00360103.............................$12.99

Country Favorites
arr. Mona Rejino
Correlates with HLSPL Level 5
00296861.............................$9.99

Disney Favorites
arr. Phillip Keveren
Correlates with HLSPL Levels 3/4
00296647.............................$10.99

Disney Film Favorites
arr. Mona Rejino
Correlates with HLSPL Level 5
00296809 ....$10.99

Disney Piano Duets
arr. Jennifer & Mike Watts
Correlates with HLSPL Level 5
00113759.............................$13.99

Double Agent! Piano Duets
arr. Jeremy Siskind
Correlates with HLSPL Level 5
00121595.............................$12.99

Easy Christmas Duets
arr. Mona Rejino & Phillip Keveren
Correlates with HLSPL Levels 3/4
00237139.............................$9.99

Easy Disney Duets
arr. Jennifer and Mike Watts
Correlates with HLSPL Level 4
00243727.............................$12.99

Four Hands on Broadway
arr. Fred Kern
Correlates with HLSPL Level 5
00146177.............................$12.99

Frozen Piano Duets
arr. Mona Rejino
Correlates with HLSPL Levels 3/4
00144294.............................$12.99

Hip-Hop for Piano Solo
arr. Logan Evan Thomas
Correlates with HLSPL Level 5
00360950.............................$12.99

Jazz Hits for Piano Duet
arr. Jeremy Siskind
Correlates with HLSPL Level 5
00143248.............................$12.99

Elton John
arr. Carol Klose
Correlates with HLSPL Level 5
00296721.............................$10.99

Joplin Ragtime Duets
arr. Fred Kern
Correlates with HLSPL Level 5
00296771.............................$8.99

Movie Blockbusters
arr. Mona Rejino
Correlates with HLSPL Level 5
00232850.............................$10.99

The Nutcracker Suite
arr. Lynda Lybeck-Robinson
Correlates with HLSPL Levels 3/4
00147906.............................$8.99

Pop Hits for Piano Duet
arr. Jeremy Siskind
Correlates with HLSPL Level 5
00224734.............................$12.99

Sing to the King
arr. Phillip Keveren
Correlates with HLSPL Level 5
00296808.............................$8.99

Smash Hits
arr. Mona Rejino
Correlates with HLSPL Level 5
00284841.............................$10.99

Spooky Halloween Tunes
arr. Fred Kern
Correlates with HLSPL Levels 3/4
00121550.............................$9.99

Today's Hits
arr. Mona Rejino
Correlates with HLSPL Level 5
00296646.............................$9.99

Top Hits
arr. Jennifer and Mike Watts
Correlates with HLSPL Level 5
00296894.............................$10.99

Top Piano Ballads
arr. Jennifer Watts
Correlates with HLSPL Level 5
00197926.............................$10.99

Video Game Hits
arr. Mona Rejino
Correlates with HLSPL Level 4
00300310.............................$12.99

You Raise Me Up
arr. Deborah Brady
Correlates with HLSPL Level 2/3
00296576.............................$7.95